Vision of the Spirit

By C. Jinarajadasa

Copyright © 2021 Lamp of Trismegistus. All rights reserved. No part of this publication may be reproduced or transmitted in any form or by any means, electronic or mechanical, including photocopying, recording, or by any information storage and retrieval system, without permission in writing from Lamp of Trismegistus. Reviewers may quote brief passages.

ISBN: 978-1-63118-560-1

Esoteric Classics

Other Books in this Series and Related Titles

Aurora of the Philosophers by Paracelsus (978-1-63118-507-6)

Clairvoyance and Psychic Abilities by A Besant &c (978-1-63118-403-1)

The Feminine Occult by various authors (978-1-63118-711-7)

Rosicrucian Rules, Secret Signs, Codes and Symbols by various (978-1-63118-488-8)

An Outline of Theosophy by C W Leadbeater (978-1-63118-452-9)

Paracelsus, the Four Elements and Their Spirits by M P Hall (978-1-63118-400-0)

The Stone of the Philosophers by A E Waite (978-1-63118-509-0)

Essays on the Esoteric Tradition of Karma by A Besant &c (978-1-63118-426-0)

The Use of Evil by Annie Besant (978-1-63118-532-8)

The Alchemical Catechism of Paracelsus by Paracelsus (978-1-63118-513-7)

Alchemy in the Nineteenth Century by Helena P Blavatsky (978-1-63118-446-8)

Qabbalistic Teachings and the Tree of Life by M P Hall (978-1-63118-482-6)

The Devil in Love by Jacques Cazotte (978–1–63118–499–4)

Fortune-Telling with Dice by Astra Cielo (978-1-63118-466-6)

History, Analysis and Secret Tradition of the Tarot by Hall &c (978-1-63118-445-1)

Crystal Vision Through Crystal Gazing by Frater Achad (978-1-63118-455-0)

The Golden Verses of Pythagoras: Five Translations (978-1-63118-479-6)

Arcane Formulas or Mental Alchemy by W W Atkinson (978-1-63118-459-8)

The Machinery of the Mind by Dion Fortune (978-1-63118-451-2)

The A E Waite Reader: A Selection of Occult Essays (978-1-63118-515-1)

The Leadbeater Reader: A Selection of Occult Essays (978-1-63118-483-3)

Audio versions are also available on Audible, Amazon and Apple

Other Books in this Series and Related Titles

On the Cave of the Nymphs in the Odyssey by Thomas Taylor (978-1-63118-505-2)

Occult Symbolism of Animals, Insects, Reptiles, Fish & Birds (978-1-63118-420-8)

The Poem of Hashish by A Crowley & C Baudelaire (978-1-63118-484-0)

Brothers & Builders by Joseph Fort Newton (978-1-63118-506-9)

The Kabbalah of Masonry & Related Writings by E Levi &c (978-1-63118-453-6)

A Collection of Fiction and Essays by Occult Writers on Supernatural and Metaphysical Subjects by various (978–1–63118–510–6)

The Sepher Yetzirah and the Qabalah by M P Hall (978-1-63118-481-9)

Kali the Mother by Sister Nivedita (978-1-63118-558-8)

The Hymns of Hermes by G R S Mead (978-1-63118-405-5)

The Secrets of Enoch by Enoch (978-1-63118-449-9)

The Hidden Mysteries of Christianity by Annie Besant (978–1–63118–534–2)

The Sword of Welleran and Other Stories by Lord Dunsany (978-1-63118-501-4)

The Eleusinian Mysteries and Rites by Dudley Wright (978–1–63118–530–4)

Gnosis of the Mind by G. R. S. Mead (978-1-63118-408-6)

The First and Second Gospels of the Infancy of Jesus Christ (978-1-63118-415-4)

The Historic, Mythic and Mystic Christ by Annie Besant (978-1-63118-533-5)

Essays on Ancient Magic by H. P. Blavatsky (978-1-63118-535-9)

Occult Arts by William Q. Judge (978-1-63118-559-5)

The Influence of Pythagoras on Freemasonry and Other Essays (978-1-63118-404-8)

The Path of Light: A Manual of Maha-Yana Buddhism (978-1-63118-471-0)

Tao Te Ching & Commentary by Lao Tzu & C Johnston (978-1-63118-495-6)

Audio versions are also available on Audible, Amazon and Apple

Table of Contents

Introduction...7

Vision of the Spirit...9
Vision of the Separated Self...17
Vision of the Mind...21
Vision of the Emotions...25
Vision of the Intuition...29
Vision of the Spirit...33

INTRODUCTION

The word "esoteric" can be difficult to define. Esotericism in general can be seen less as a system of beliefs and more as a category, which encompasses numerous, different systems of beliefs. It's a bit of juxtaposition, since the word "esoteric" indicates something that few people know about, while the term itself broadly covers numerous philosophies, practices, areas of study and belief systems.

In a greater sense, Esotericism acts as a storehouse for secret knowledge, which is often considered ancient (by *tradition, if not by fact),* passed down from generation to generation, in private. At various times in history, simply possessing the knowledge of some of these subjects, was considered illegal and a jailable offence, if discovered. This usually included such general topics as Alchemy, Pharmacology, Qabalah, Hermeticism, Occultism, Ceremonial Magic, Astrology, Divination, Rosicrucianism and so on. Collectively, these areas of study were often referred to as the esoteric sciences.

Sometimes, the outer garment of a subject isn't esoteric, while what is hidden beneath it, is. As an example, Freemasonry isn't necessarily esoteric by nature (at *least not anymore),* but certain signs, passwords and handshakes given to the candidate during their initiation, are in fact, esoteric, in the sense that they are hidden from the general public.

Today, in the twenty-first century, such topics are readily available at bookstores across the country, and numerous mainsteam publishers offer beginners guides and coffee-table volumes on many of these subjects, intended for mass appeal. Books like *"The Secret"* have turned previously arcane topics into household knowledge. All that being the case, however, it isn't to say that there still aren't buried secrets to uncover, ancient wisdom being ignored and forgotten mysteries to be explored. In fact, it is often that we are only able to further our own studies by standing on the shoulders of these disappearing giants.

Lamp of Trismegistus is doing its part to help preserve humanity's esoteric history by making some of these classics available to those students who are seeking to unearth the knowledge of these ancient colossi.

So, be sure to check other titles from our *Esoteric Classics* series, as well as our *Occult Fiction*, *Theosophical Classics*, *Foundations of Freemasonry Series*, *Supernatural Fiction*, *Paranormal Research Series*, *Studies in Buddhism* and our *Christian Apocrypha Series*. You can also download the audio versions of most of these titles from Amazon, Apple or Audible, for learning on the go.

THE VISION OF THE SPIRIT

The history of humanity is the history of ideas, and the stages through which men have risen from savage to civilized are distinguishable one from the other by the influence of certain great doctrines. Among these teachings that have molded civilizations, the idea of Evolution stands out as heralding a new era in the world of thought. Considered at first as of more academic interest, soon it was recognized as of practical value, and today it is known as necessary in the understanding of every problem in every department of being.

Nevertheless it is a fact that the doctrine of evolution is a theory after all. No one has lived long enough to see sufficient links in the evolutionary chain to attest that the changes postulated as having taken place actually did so occur, and that the chain is not a fancy but a fact. Yet evolution is accepted by all as a dynamic idea, for like a magic wand it performs wonders in the world of thought. It marshals the heterogeneous organisms of nature into orderly groups, and from inanimate element to protoplasm, from unicellular organism to multi cellular, from invertebrate to vertebrate, from ape to man, one ascending scale of life is seen.

> *And striving to be man, the worm*
> *Mounts through all the spires of form.*

Yet none can say that evolution is an agreeable fact to contemplate, for there is a ruthlessness to nature's methods that is appalling. Utterly cruel and wasteful she seems, creating and perfecting her creatures only to prey on each other, generating more than can live in the fierce struggle for existence; "red in tooth and claw," she builds and unbuilds and builds again, one-pointed only that a type shall survive and reckless of the pleasure or pain to a single life. Men themselves, proud though they be in a fancied freedom of thought and action, are nothing but pawns in a game she plays. The more fully evolution is understood from such facts as scientists have so far gathered, the more justifiably can men say with Omar of their birth, life, and death:

> *Into this Universe, and Why not knowing,*
> *Nor Whence, like Water willy-nilly flowing,*
> *And out of it, like Wind along the Waste,*
> *I know not Whither, willy-nilly blowing.*

Of course this attitude does not represent that of the majority of men. Millions of men believe in a Creator and that "God's in His heaven, all's right with the world!" But it is no exaggeration to say that their optimism continually receives rude shocks. No man or woman of sensibility can look about him and not agree with Tennyson's comparison of life to a play.

> *Act first, this earth, a stage so gloom'd with woe*
> *You all but sicken at the shifting scenes.*
> *And yet be patient. Our Playwright may show*
> *In some fifth Act what this wild Drama means.*

Both the idea of evolution and the idea of a Divine Guidance, as at present conceived, fail to satisfy fully the needs of men for an inspiring view of life. The former indeed shows a splendid pageant of nature, but it has no message to individual man except to make the most of his brief day of life, and stoically resign himself to extinction when nature shall have no further use for him. The latter speaks to men's hearts in alluring accents of a power that maketh for righteousness, but it sees God as existing only in the gaps of that pitiless cosmic order that science reveals. It is obvious, therefore, that any philosophy which postulates an inseparable relation between God and evolution, between nature and man, is worthy of examination, and this is the view of life that Theosophy propounds in the light of one great idea.

This idea is that of the Evolution of Life. Just as modern science tells us of a ceaseless change of forms from protoplasm to man, so Theosophy asserts that there is, *pari passu,* a changing, growing life. This life does not depend on the forms, though we see it associated with them; and of it Theosophy says that first it is indestructible, and second that it evolves.

It is indestructible, in the sense that when an organism is destroyed, nevertheless all is not destroyed, for there remains a life that is still conscious. If a rose fades and its petals crumble and fall into dust, the *life* of that rose has not therefore ceased to be; that life persists in nature, retaining in itself all the memories of all the experiences it gained garbed as a rose. Then in due course of events, following laws that are comprehensible, that life animates another rose of another spring, bringing to its second embodiment the memories of its first. Whenever therefore there seems the death of a living thing, crystal or plant, animal or man, there persists an indestructible life and consciousness, even though to all appearance the object is lifeless and processes of decay have begun.

Further, this life is evolving in exactly the same way that the scientist says that an organism evolves. The life is at first amorphic, responding but little to the stimuli from without, retaining only feeble memories of the experiences it gains through its successive embodiments. But it passes from stage to stage through more and more complex organisms, till slowly it becomes more definite, more diverse in its functions; as the outer form evolves from protoplasm to man, so evolves too the life ensouling it. All nature, visible and invisible, is the field of an evolution of life through successive series of evolving forms, and the broad stages of this evolving life are from mineral to vegetable, from vegetable to animal, and from animal to man.

The doctrine of a life that evolves through evolving forms answers some of those questions that puzzle the biologist today. Many a fact hitherto considered as outside the domain of science is seen as illustrative of new laws, and existing gaps are bridged over to make the doctrine of evolution more logical than ever. It further shows nature as not wasteful and only seemingly cruel, for nothing is lost, and every experience in every form that was destroyed in the process of natural selection is treasured by the life today. The past lives in the present to attest that nature's purpose is not death crushing life, but life ever triumphant over death to make out of stocks and stones immortal men.

In each human being is seen this same principle of an imperishable evolving life. For man is an individual life and consciousness, an immortal soul capable of living apart from the body we usually call 'the man'. In each soul the process of evolution is at work, for at his entrance on existence as a soul, he is feeble and chaotic in his consciousness, vague and indefinite in his understanding of the meaning of life, and capable only of a narrow range of thought and feeling. But he too evolves, from indefinite to definite, from simple to complex, from chaos to order.

Man's evolution is by successive manifestations in bodies of flesh, passing at the death of one body to begin life once more in another new one; and in this passage he carries with him the memory of all experiences he has gained in the past behind him. This aspect of the evolution of life as it affects men is called reincarnation.

As all processes of nature are intelligible on the hypothesis of an evolution of organisms, so all that happens to men becomes comprehensible in the light of reincarnation; as the former links all forms by species and genus, family and order, class and group, sub-kingdom and kingdom into one unbreakable chain, so the latter binds all human experiences into one consistent philosophy of life. How reincarnation explains the mysteries around us and inspires us we shall now see.

Imagine with me that existence is a mountain, and that millions are climbing to its summit. Let many days be needed before a traveler comes to his goal. Then as he climbs day after day, the proportion of things below him and above him will change; new sights will greet his eyes, new airs will breathe around him; his eyes will adjust themselves to new horizons, and step by step objects will change shape and proportion. At last on reaching the summit a vast panorama will extend before him, and he will see clearly every part of the road he climbed, and why it dipped into this valley and circled that crag. Let this mountain typify existence, and let the climbers up its sides be men and women who are immortal souls.

Let us now think for a moment of travelers at the mountain's base, who are to climb to its summit. We know how limited must be their horizon and how little they can see of the long path before them. Let such travelers typify the most backward of our humanity, the most savage and least intelligent men and women we can find today. According to reincarnation these are child-souls, just entering into existence to undergo evolution and to be made into perfect souls. To understand the process of evolution let us watch one of them stage by stage as he climbs the mountain.

The first thing that we shall note is that this child-soul manifests a duality. For he is soul and body; as a soul he is from God but as a body he is from the brute.

The Lord let the house of a brute to the soul of a man,
And the man said, Am I your debtor?

*And the Lord, Not yet, but make it an clean as you can,
And then I will let you a better.*

The body he occupies has in it a strong instinct of self-preservation, stamped upon it by the fierce struggle for existence of its animal progenitors; he himself as a soul coming from God has intuitions as to right and wrong, but as yet hardly any will. The body demands for its preservation that he be self-assertive and selfish; lacking the will to direct his evolution he acts as the body impels.

THE VISION OF THE SEPARATED SELF

Hence at this earliest stage of the soul his vision of life as he climbs is that of the separated self. 'Mine not yours' is his principle of action; greed rules him and a thirst for sensation drives him on, and he little heeds that he is unjust and cruel to others as he lives through his nights and days of selfishness and self- assertion. He seems strong-willed, for he crushes the weaker before him; but in reality he has no will at all, for he is but the plaything of an animal heredity he cannot control. He has no more freedom of will than the water-wheel that turns at the bidding of the descending stream; he is but the tool of a 'will to live' that accomplishes a purpose not his own.

Millions of men and women around us are at this first stage. Their craftiness, hardly deserving the name of intellect, is that of a Falstaff for whom "the world is mine oyster which I with sword will open". In their least animal phases comfort is their aim in life: "They dressed, digested, talked, articulated words; other vitality showed they almost none." The universe around them is meaningless, and they are scarce capable of wonder: "Let but a Rising of the Sun, let but a creation of the world happen twice, and it ceases to be marvelous, to be noteworthy or noticeable." The center of the circle of the cosmos is in themselves and they neither know nor care if another and truer center be possible.

Yet when we recognize that each of these souls is immortal and that his future is "the future of a thing whose growth and splendor have no limit," we begin to understand why at this early stage selfishness plays such a prominent part in his life. For in the stages to come he must be capable of standing alone, firm on the basis of a coherent individuality; now it is, therefore, he must develop initiative and strength. He is quick to retaliate, but the germs of swift decision are grown thereby; he is domineering and cruel, but the seeds of intelligent enterprise result from the animal cunning he displays. Every evil he does must sometime be paid back in laborious service to his victims; yet on the whole the evil he does at this stage is less in quantity and force, for all its seeming, than that done in later stages where intelligence is keener and emotion more powerful. At a certain period in human evolution selfishness has its place in the economy of things, for selfishness too is a force used to build the battlements of heaven.

These souls, whose youth alone is the cause of their selfishness, are in their essence divine, and there is in them no evil of a positive kind; the vices are but the result of the absence of virtues, and the evil "is null, is naught, is silence implying sound". Each is a 'good man' who, deep down within him, has a knowledge of "the one true way," though in his attempts to tread it he seems to retrograde rather than to evolve. Like plants in a garden they are all tended by Him from whom they come; lie knows the perfect souls that he will make out of them by change and growth as the ages pass by.

Though still confused his service unto Me,
I soon shall lend him to a clearer morning.
Sees not the gardener, even while he buds his tree,

Both flower and fruit the future years adorning?

Life after life these souls come to birth, now as men and now as women; they live a life of selfishness, and they die, and hardly any change will be noticeable in the character; but slowly there steals into their lives a dissatisfaction. The mind is too dull to grasp the relation of the individual to the whole, and the imagination is too feeble to realize that "man doth not live by bread alone." Hence it is that "the thousand natural shocks that flesh is heir to" are duly marshaled and employed to ruffle their self-centered contentment; old age and death cast over them shadows that have no power to sadden a philosophic mind; disease and accident lie in wait for them to weigh down their spirits and make them rebel against a fate they do not understand. Till their hearts shall enshrine a divine purpose, a Hound of Heaven pursues them, and "naught shall shelter thee, that wilt not shelter Me."

Thus are they made ready to pass on to the next stage; the foundations of abilities have been laid, and the individual is firm on a basis built through selfishness. Now has come the time to begin the laborious work of casting out the self, and so there opens before the soul's gaze the vision of the next stage. According to the type of soul, this vision is either the Vision of the Mind or the Vision of the Emotions.

There are in life two main types of souls, the one in whom intelligence controls emotion and the other in whom emotion sways the mind. One type is not more evolved than the other; they are both stages to pass through to grow a higher faculty, that of Intuition. The vision of the third stage is the Vision of the Intuition, but to it souls come from the first stage either through intellect or through emotion. Let us first consider those souls whose evolution is by way of the intellect.

THE VISION OF THE MIND

We shall see in the past of these souls that much intelligence has been developed in the first stage; their selfishness has made them quick and cunning to adapt opportunities to minister to their comfort. This intelligence is now taken up by the unseen Guides of evolution, and the soul is placed in environments that will change mere animal cunning into true intellect. The past good and evil sown by him will be adjusted in its reaping, so as to give him occupations and interests that will force him to think of men and things around him apart from their relation to himself. Instead of weighing experiences in terms of personal comfort he begins now to group them in types and categories; little by little he begins to see a material and moral order in the cosmos that is more powerful than his will. Each law of nature when first seen is feared by him, for it seems to be there to thwart him; but later, with more experience of its working, he begins to trust it and to depend upon it to achieve his aim. A love of learning appears in him and nature is no longer a blank page; he has ceased to be "a pair of spectacles behind which there is no eye."

At this stage we shall see that the selfishness still in him will warp the judgments of his mind. He will be a doctrinaire, a pedant, combative and full of prejudice; for all his intellect his character will show marked weaknesses, and will often see and propound principles of conduct which he will not be able to apply to himself. Again and again he will fail to see how little he understands the world, since the world is the embodiment of a life that is more than mind, and whoso understands it with mind alone will misunderstand. Excess of intellect will become in him defect of intelligence, and he will see all things as through a glass darkly.

Many a life will pass while he slowly gains experiences through the mind and assimilates them into a truer conception of life. By now he will have begun to take part in the intellectual life of the world, and when he is on the threshold of the next stage we shall find him as a worker in science, philosophy or literature. But his intellect has too great a personal bias still, and it must be made impersonal and pure before the next vision, that of the intuition, can be his. Once again we shall see that there enters into his life a dissatisfaction. The structures which he builds so laboriously as the results of years of work will crumble one by one, because nature reveals new facts to show the world that his generalizations were only partly true; the world for which he toiled will forget him and younger workers will receive the honors that are his due. He will be misunderstood by his dearest friends, and "he is now, if not ceasing, yet intermitting to eat his own heart, and clutches round him outwardly on the Not-Me for wholesomer food."

But this suffering, though the reaping of sad sowings of injustice to others through prejudice brings in its train a high purification sooner or later; the soul learns the great lesson of working for work's sake and not for the fruit of action. Now he knows the joy of altruistic dedication of himself to the search of truth. A student of philosophies but the slave of none, he now watches nature as it is, and in a perfect impersonality of mind solves her mysteries one by one of him now can it be said with the Pythagoreans that "a great intellect is the chorus of divinity." Thus dawns for him the Vision of the Intuition.

THE VISION OF THE EMOTIONS

I mentioned when describing the transition from the first stage to the second that there were in the world two main types of souls - those who pass from the Vision of the Separated Self to the Vision of the Intuition by way of the mind, and those others who develop along a parallel path and pass from the emotions to the intuition. We have just seen how souls are trained through intellect to cast out the self; we shall now see how the same result is achieved for those in whom emotions sway the mind.

As the intellectual type showed in the first stage a marked development of intelligence of a low kind, so similarly shall we find that the souls we are going to consider show during the same stage a great deal of feeling. Not that this feeling will be refined or unselfish; indeed it will mostly be lust and jealousy, with perhaps a little crude religious emotion in addition. But the character will be obviously easily swayed by emotions, and this trait in the soul is now taken up and worked upon to enable him to pass to the next stage.

Following his emotional bent, and selfish and oblivious of the feelings of those around him, the soul will compel others weaker than himself to be the slaves of his desires; but the passion and the sense of possession he has of these that minister to his lusts will link him to them life after life, till slowly he begins to feel that they are necessary to his emotional life and not dispensable at will. Gradually his impure passions will be transformed into purer affections, and then he will be brought again and again into contact with them so that his emotions shall go out impulsively towards them. But the evil he wrought them in the past will now cast a veil over their eyes and make them indifferent to him. He will be forced to love on, to atone for past evil by service, but despair will be the only reward; when in resentment he tries to break the bond that ties him to them he will find he cannot. He will curse love, only to return again to again to love's altar with his offerings.

Though life now becomes full of disappointment and despair, in his serener moments he will acknowledge that in spite of the suffering it entailed, his emotional life has slowly opened a new sense in him. He catches now and then glimpses of an undying youth in all things, and the world that seems dreary and aging will re-appear under certain emotional stress as he knew it before life became a tragedy. These glimpses are transitory at first, lasting indeed only so long as the love emotion colors his being; but there is for him a time:

> *When all the world is young, lad,*
> *And all the trees are green,*
> *And every goose a swan, lad,*
> *And every lass a queen.*

Life after life, fostered by his transitory loves, this sense will grow in him till it blossoms into a sense of wonder. Then nature reveals in all things in life new values whose significance he can henceforth never wholly forget. While love sways his being each blade of grass and leaf and flower has to him a new meaning; he sees beauty now where he saw none before. Everything beautiful around him - a face, a flower, a sunset, a melody - will link him in mysterious ways to those he loves; the world ceases to be a blank page.

> *Love wakes men once a lifetime each,*
> *They lift their heavy lids and look ;*
> *And lo! what one sweet page can teach,*
> *They read with joy, then close the book.*
> *And some give thanks, and some blaspheme,*
> *And most forget. But either way*
> *That and the child's unheeded dream*
> *Is all the light of all their day.*

It will happen that this sense of wonder is intermittent, and that there come periods when the world is veiled; but the veil is of his own making, and must be torn asunder if he is to possess the Vision of the Intuition. Once more there enters into his life a dissatisfaction - a discontent that love itself is transitory after all. Those he loves and who love him in return will be taken from him just when life seems in flower; friends he idealizes will shatter the ideals so lovingly made of them. Cruel as it all seems, it is but the reaping of sad sowings in past lives, but the reaping has a meaning now as always. He has so far been loving not Love but its shadow, not the Ideal from which nothing can be taken away but its counterfeit which suffers diminution; he must now see clearer and feel truer. The character must be steadied so that it shall not rebound from enthusiasm to depression, nor be satisfied with a vague mysticism that prefers to revel in its own feelings rather than evaluate what causes them.

Hence the inevitable purification through suffering; the dross of self is burned away till there remains the gold of a divine desire. He then discovers that the truest feelings are only those that have in them the spirit of offering. Now for him thus purified in desire and for that other type of soul made impersonal in intellect there dawns the Vision of the Intuition.

THE VISION OF THE INTUITION

"Before the eyes can see, they must be incapable of tears. Before the ear can hear, it must have lost its sensitiveness." All souls that have come to this stage have learnt by now the bitter lesson that "it is only with Renunciation that Life, properly speaking, can be said to begin"; they have proved in their own experience that what once seemed death was but a "repentance unto life." They have now discovered the meaning of life - that man is a child of God come forth to life to be a co-worker with his Father. It matters not that a soul does not state to himself his relation to the whole in these terms; it only matters that he should have discovered that his part in existence is to be a worker in a work, and that nothing happening to himself matters so long as that work proceeds to its inevitable end. He knows that the end of thought and feeling is action for his fellow-men, and that this action must be either dispassionate and without thought of reward, or full of a spirit of grateful offering.

He possesses now the faculty of the intuition, which transcending both reason and emotion yet can justify its judgments to either, he grows past 'common-sense,' the criterion for common things, into an uncommon sense; for life is full now of uncommon things of whose existence others are not aware. In men and women he discerns those invisible factors which are inevitable in human relations, and hence his judgment of them is "not of this world." In all things he sees and feels One Life. Whatever unites attracts him; if intellectual he will love to synthesize in science or philosophy, if emotional he will dedicate himself to art or philanthropy.

Now slowly for him the Many become the One. The Unity will be known only in the vision of the next stage, but preparing him for it, science and art, religion and philosophy, will deduce for him eternal fundamental types from the kaleidoscope of life. Types of forms, types of thought, types of emotions, types of temperament - these he sees everywhere round him, and life in all its phases becomes transformed because it reflects as in a mirror Archetypes of a realm beyond time and space and mutability.

> *Everything of mortal birth*
> *- Is but a type;*
> *What was of feeble worth*
> *- Here becomes ripe.*
> *What was a mystery*
> *- Here meets the eye;*
> *The Ever-womanly*
> *- Draws us on high.*

'The Ever-womanly' now shows him everywhere one Wisdom; science tells him of the oneness of nature and philosophy that man is a consciousness creating his world; art reveals in all things youth and beauty and religion whispers to his heart that Love broods over all. His sympathies go to all as his will is ever at their service.

Not far now is the time when for him shall dawn the vision of the Spirit. But to bring him to its portal a dissatisfaction once more enters his soul. No longer can that dissatisfaction be personal; the sad reaping of sorrow for evil done is over, and "only the sorrow of others casts its shadow over me". Nor is it caused by any sense of the mutability of things, for, absolutely, without question, he knows his immortality, and that though all things change there is behind them that which changes never. Yet while he climbs to his appointed goal dissatisfaction must always be.

It comes to him now as a creator. For with intuition to guide him he creates in that field of endeavor in which he has trained himself in past lives; as poet, artist, statesman, saint, or scientist, he is one of the world's geniuses. But though his creations are a miracle to all, yet to him they are only partly true and only partly beautiful, for he sees the ideal which he would fain bring down to men, and knows his failure as none others can know. Life is teaching him "to attain by shadowing forth the unattainable."

As thus he grows life after life, scientist and poet, artist and saint now merge into a new type of being who sees with " larger, other eyes than ours." He has regained his integrity of heart and his innocence of hands and is become "a little child"; "by pity enlightened" he is now Parsifal, "the Pure Fool," who enters upon his heritage.

THE VISION OF THE SPIRIT

Then it is that at its threshold there meets him One who has watched him climbing for many a life and all unseen has encouraged him. This is the Master, one of that "goodliest fellowship of famous knights whereof the world holds record." In him the soul sees in realization all those ideals that have drawn him onward and upward; and hand in hand with this "Father in God" he now treads the way while the Vision of the Spirit is shown him by his Master. Who shall describe that vision but those that have it, and how may one less than a Master here speak with authority? And yet since Masters of the Wisdom have moved among men, since Buddha, Krishna and Christ have shown us in Their lives something of what that vision is, surely from their lives we can deduce what the vision must be.

In that Vision of the Spirit the Many is the One. "Alone within this universe he comes and goes; 'tis He who is the fire, the water He pervadeth; Him and Him only knowing, one crosseth over death; no other path at all is there to go."

Now for the soul who has come to the end of his climbing each man is only "the spirit he worked in, not what he did, but what he became." There is no high nor low in life, for in all he sees a ray from the Divine Flame; as through the highest so through the lowest too, to him "God stooping shows sufficient of His light for us in the dark to rise by." Life is henceforth become a Sacrament and he is its Celebrant; with loving thoughts and deeds he celebrates and at-ones man with God and God with man. He discerns, purifies in himself, and offers to God "infinite passion and the pain of finite hearts that yearn"; from God on high he brings to men what alone can satisfy that yearning.

He has renounced "the will to live" and thereby has made its purpose his own: "Foregoing self the universe grows I." Yet he knows with rapture that that 'I' is but a tiny lens in a great Light. Henceforth he lives only that a Greater than he may live through him, love through him, act through him; and evermore shall his heart whisper, in heaven or in hell, whithersoever his work may take him: "Him know I, the Mighty Man, resplendent like the Sun, beyond the Darkness; Him and him only knowing one crosseth over death; no other path at all is there to go."

Thus do we, the happy few, the precursors of a new age, see life in the light of reincarnation. As the evolutionist sees all nature linked in one ladder of life, and sky and sea testify to him of evolution, so do we see all men linked in one common purpose, and their hopes and fears, their self-sacrifice and their selfishness, testify to us of reincarnation. Life and its experiences have ceased to be for us

> *An arch where thro'*
> *Gleams that untravell'd world, whose margin fades*
> *For ever and for ever when I move*
> *No longer can the world be for us as the poet sang:*
> *Act first, this earth, a stage so gloom'd with woe*

You all but sicken at the shifting scenes.
And yet be patient. Our Playwright may show
In some fifth Act what this wild drama means.

    The Fifth Act is here before our eyes. It is that Vision of the Spirit that is the heritage of every soul and thither all men are slowly treading for "no other path at all is there to go."

www.ingramcontent.com/pod-product-compliance
Lightning Source LLC
LaVergne TN
LVHW041503070426
835507LV00009B/795